#BeatMolestation

MW01627715

NO MORE SECRETS

Aprille,
I am so proud
of you! Thank you
for walking in your
greatness and bringing us
(ss) along for the ride! You
are amazing! Hold on... the
best is yet to come! I am
excited to see what is next!
Love you, Cam! Stay Epic!
XO

NO MORE SECRETS

How to Discuss Molestation with Your Children

MISHONDY WRIGHT-BROWN

NO MORE SECRETS

Limits of Liability and Disclaimer of Warranty

The author and publisher shall not be liable for your misuse of this material. This book is strictly for informational and educational purposes. The author and/or publisher do not guarantee that anyone following these techniques, suggestions, tips, ideas, or strategies will become successful. The author and/or publisher shall have neither liability nor responsibility to anyone with respect to any loss or damage caused, or alleged to be caused, directly or indirectly by the information contained in this book

Published by: Purposely Created Publishing Group™

Printed in the United States of America

ISBN (ebook) 978-1-942838-61-6

ISBN (paperback) 978-1-942838-60-9

TABLE OF CONTENTS

DEDICATION

For my loves, Tanéa, Kayla, and Teej.

Thank you for forgiving me for not recognizing the signs. Thank you for giving me permission to go forward. You volunteered to share your Mommy and your stories with the world. You three complete me.

For all of the children who will experience life without molestation because of this book: You deserve a fair shot. I will fight forever for you to get it. You deserve it!

For the end to child molestation.

By giving away pieces of myself,
I have somehow become whole...

INTRODUCTION

"It is easier to build strong children than to repair broken men" - Frederick Douglass

SECRET:

a: kept from knowledge or view

b: marked by the habit of discretion

You are reading these words, so it is safe to say that you want to talk with your child about molestation.

I realize that it is hard; molestation is not the topic any parent wishes to discuss at the dinner table with their child. With all of the things that you want and need to tell your child, I am quite sure that the talk about molestation is the furthest thing from your mind. I was in the same place, but there came a point in my parenting where I felt that I needed to have the talk with my children. I thought about it long and hard beforehand.

As a survivor of multiple molestations, I knew that it was something that I needed to discuss with my babies. However, no one told me how, when, or where to conduct this much-needed chat. All I had was the 'why'—my children were not, under any circumstances, going to be subjected to the horrific pain of being molested.

I am writing this book to give you an effective way to discuss molestation with your children. As you will see, I really could have benefited from having a tool such as this. Let us empower our children. They need it.

Mishondy

"It takes a village to raise a child." - African Proverb

Chapter 1

Why Should I Discuss Molestation with My Child?

"No one ever keeps a secret so well as a child"
- Victor Hugo

According to the American Medical Association, 20 percent of all victims [of molestation] develop serious, long term psychological problems.

You may ask yourself this question quite a few times before you actually have the discussion. That is to be expected; you probably feel like you do not need to have this conversation with your baby. After all, you are very active in your child's life. You probably never ever allow them to spend the night at a friend's house, you attend all of their games and practices, and you spend your summers on family vacations, together, so you are never away from your child. Your precious baby is always within your eyesight, right? Wrong.

Unfortunately, child molesters are everywhere. They do not wear any identifiers—at least none that are obvious to the untrained, unsuspecting eye. They are your child's coaches, teachers, pastors, cousins, uncles, aunts, babysitters, brothers, sisters...dad.

You may have even had some semblance of a conversation about "good touch, bad touch" with your child. That is a great place to start. But, if you are like I was, you made threats...um, promises...about what you would do to anyone who would DARE touch your child. Your description of what would occur was probably crystal clear!

After the conversation, you probably felt pretty good about having had the talk. After all, the dreaded conversation is over; you feel as though you have equipped your child with the tools to ward off any potential molestation. The problem is this: now, your child is afraid for anyone who may even think of touching them. And, they are afraid that if someone does touch them, you will do as you promised them you would do. At this point, your child would not tell you about their "bad touch" because they have to protect you and their predator. Yes, they protect the predator because that person is, more than likely, very close to them.

That is just too much for any child to handle alone, so naturally your child becomes silent. Is that what you want, as a parent, for your child to carry around the burden of an attempted attack (or, heaven forbid, an actual attack) without having anyone to talk with about it? I can answer that question for you. You would not want your child to be silent about something that could potentially destroy their lives.

Victims of child molestation who never get a chance to talk about their experiences oftentimes become involved in things that are detrimental to their well-being. Most victims experience depression, feelings of shame and guilt, suicidal ideations, promiscuity, and low self-esteem—just to name a few things. As a survivor of child molestation, I know exactly how this feels. As a parent of children who have been molested, I understand the importance of discussing molestation with your children.

I have watched how molestation can completely alter the course of a child's life. It changes everything. A child is robbed of their innocence.

Having the conversation with your child is extremely

important. I believe that child molestation is preventable but only through the empowerment of children and the education of the adults who have the charge of protecting these children, which is why we *have* to talk to them.

"When you learn, teach." - Ethiopian Proverb

I thought I had it all figured out. The things that happened to me as a child were not going to happen to my children. I planned this time to talk with my children about molestation; you know, I knew exactly what I was going to say to them. I remember it like it was yesterday. It was a Saturday, and my three children were sitting in the living room on the sofa. The early afternoon sun was peeking through the blinds. I took a deep breath, put on my game face, and I proceeded to talk with my children about molestation. I told them what I would do to anyone who ever touched them. I think I said a few things about "good touch, bad touch," but not nearly enough.

I remember their eyes were open wide and fixed on me (probably because I was looking like a crazed woman). They sat listening to me as I paced back and forth across our living room floor, trying to get to the end of this conversation that I was reluctant to have with them. They sat next to their father as I gave way too many details on what I would do if anyone ever thought about touching them. They all stared at me with fear in their faces! At that moment, my middle daughter asked me, with the sweetest little voice, "Can't we just call 911?"

That little voice of reason. If I knew then what I now know, I would have understood that my daughter was offering me an alternative way of dealing with her future molestation that was far better than what I had suggested. I would have revisited the topic of molestation on another day with a totally different approach. I allowed my past experiences and fear to interfere with my ability to truly protect my children. I explained to my children a horrific scenario that was from the little girl within me who, having been molested multiple times, was still seeking justice. My pain clouded my judgment. My precious little girl was already worried about what would happen to her future molester if she uttered one word of her attacks to her Monster Mommy. Children are afraid of monsters. Monsters do not help us prevent molestation.

But education and empowerment do! My experiences and the experiences of others, with whom I have encountered, have taught me that we can prevent molestation! As much as we want to keep our children safe from the darkness of the big, bad world, we handicap them by keeping them sheltered from the things that they will more than likely encounter. According to www.RAINN.org, 1 out of 3 girls and 1 out of 5 boys will be molested by the age of 18. Those are only the numbers that we know of. I am in the number of unreported cases. So is my brother. So is my mother, aunt, and several of my friends. This lets me know that being approached by a predator is something that almost every child will experience.

Why not give them the tools to stop it before it starts?

One day, I decided to talk to my children about the birds and the bees. I had prepared for this day for years. It was another uneasy conversation that I knew that I needed to have with my children, but I was determined to make it a successful one. I sat the three of them down and said, "Tell me what you know about sex." They looked at one another, and my son blurted out, "We know about sex, Mommy. Dad showed us movies." My heart dropped. The "movies" that my son was referring to were pornographic movies. I took a deep breath, swallowed (my anger) hard and asked them to describe to me how they had movie night. My son proceeded to tell me that his dad played the movies and watched them with him, with the room darkened.

He remembered his dad watching him and not the movie. He asked him how watching the movie made him feel. He sat beside him. No popcorn, no soft drinks. Just my baby, his dad, and the movie. He was about 6 years old. My daughters spoke of him sitting on my oldest daughter's bed, lights dimmed, and making them watch the movies to "...teach them about sex..." I did not know how to respond because at that time, I did not know that watching pornographic movies with a child was molestation. I do now.

Still not sure that you should have this conversation with your children? Still on the fence about whether or not they can handle it? They can. We start teaching our children foreign languages in Pre-K—some even start in the womb! We are teaching them how to read as soon as they can speak. They are super smart, and they can take it. Maybe after this story, you will be inclined to have the conversation with your child.

She is my first born. Beautiful, brilliant, and deaf. Profoundly deaf. That did not stop this child at all! As a child, she was a sponge—absorbing everything that crossed her path. I was extremely protective of each of my children, but I was more protective of her. She could not hear what was going on in the world, so it was my job to protect her from dangers unheard.

She recalled lying in bed, asleep, on her side. She did not hear her father slide in the bed beside her. She could not hear his moans and groans as he attempted to penetrate his own daughter. She recalled feeling him and jumping because she did not know, nor did she understand, what was happening. She said that he went into the bathroom afterward. Because I wanted to be certain that I understood what she was explaining, I asked her to demonstrate. I excused myself to the bathroom to vomit.

Take action now!

When will you have the conversation with your child?

____

____

____

Chapter 2

What is Molestation?

"Nothing quite encourages as does one's first unpunished crime." - Marquis de Sade

Before we can begin to have a discussion with our children about molestation, we must first know exactly what molestation is. When I had the (what I believed to be) effective conversation about molestation with my children, I did not know what I know now. I knew that touching the genitals and penetration were examples of molestation, but that was the extent of my knowledge.

Even though I had already survived multiple incidences of molestation, my knowledge was limited to *my* experiences with molestation. I went into the fight without the proper artillery.

You would be surprised at the number of educated child specialists who do not know all that molestation entails. As I have conducted workshops and shared my story, I see more light bulbs go off when I give the rundown on what molestation is. Because I have witnessed so many 'aha' moments when I have shared this information, I will spend this chapter going over the monster that is molestation.

So what, exactly, is molestation?

Molestation is any unwanted sexual act, which includes touching and non-touching activity. It includes any sexual act between an adult and a minor or between two minors when one exerts power over the other. It also includes non-physical acts such as exhibitionism, exposure to pornography, voyeurism and communicating in a sexual manner by phone or Internet. Pretty clear, right? Think about this:

Tommy is recognized by those in his community as a great father. He is always seen spending time with his children. One day, when his wife is not at home, he asks one of the neighborhood boys to come over to his house. He then tells his oldest daughter (who is about 10 years old) to kiss this boy. He stands with them and instructs them to kiss longer. He then tells them how to kiss deeper. He continues to watch. His rationale for this act: he said that he was teaching his daughter how to behave when she gets a boyfriend.

Was she molested? Was the boy? Absolutely! Voyeurism is a form of molestation. The predator is getting sexual gratification from watching two children perform an unwanted, unsolicited sexual act. Why would an adult feel the need to teach a 10-year-old child about relationships in this manner?

What about this:

A child is visiting her favorite aunt and uncle for the summer. She just loves going to spend her summers with them! Since she is one of five children, she enjoys the chance to be the 'only child.' One evening, while she is outside playing, her uncle comes to her and tells her to come inside in 10 minutes. He tells her that he and her aunt will be in the bedroom watching movies and for her to come to the bedroom and let them know that she was inside. When she gets to the bedroom, the door is slightly closed, but her uncle sees her. He is having sex with her aunt. She does not see the girl, but he does. He smiles at her and continues to have sex with his wife.

Was the little girl molested? Yes! The uncle, more than likely, was grooming the little girl for a future attack. He was sexually gratified by having his niece watch him have sex. This is called exhibitionism.

See how molestation does not necessarily involve touching? Although those scenarios may have been detailed, it is imperative that we take a candid look at this monster in order to defeat it! Before we go any further with examples of molestation, let us look at how a predator may behave before they go for the kill.

The predator usually begins by trying to gain a child's trust. They throw out little tests to see if the child is going to notice that they are being baited or if the child will not see them coming. They start with something that, if the child reported it to someone, has the ability to be interpreted as a completely innocent act. They want to see if the child will keep their secret.

Most of the time, the child is not equipped with the tools to recognize what is about to take place. At this point, the predator may be offering them back rubs, tickling them, wrestling with them, or telling jokes with a sexual undertone.

Once they see that the child is comfortable with these little tests, the predator continues with their game. At this point, they may touch/fondle the child, show them pornographic images/videos, send them sexually explicit text messages/pictures, or engage in masturbation/intercourse with the child. They usually will not hurt the child because they feel as though a child will inform their parent(s) if they are injured in any way.

Now back to defining molestation. Molestation can be kissing, fondling, touching, showing pornographic images, voyeurism, exhibitionism, showing genitals to a child—any unwanted sexual act. If the other person can get sexual gratification from the act, it is molestation. We need to know that because predators may tell the child that there is nothing wrong with what they are doing since it is not overtly sexual. In the midst of the child's confusion, the predator continues on with his or her task at hand.

Bella loves playing hide-and-seek! Even while you are preparing dinner, she is telling you, "Count, Mommy! Come and find me!" It is during the holiday season, and you have family over. You are in the kitchen cooking and, as usual, Bella tells you to "Count, Mommy!" You dismiss her with a wave of the hand, and Bella seems disappointed. Her cousin Byron, who is visiting from out of town, says to her, "I'll play with you." She is excited to play her favorite game and goes to hide. Byron finds her and starts to tickle her. The mom hears her laughing hysterically. Later, she sees that Bella is sitting on Byron's lap. She looks over, and Byron smiles at her. So does Bella, so she thinks that everything is okay. Meanwhile, he is 'dancing' while she sits on his lap.

In this scenario, was Bella molested? Sure she was! The predator was able to get away with it because he was doing it right under her mother's nose. He was first able to get Bella's attention by participating in something that she enjoyed. With that, he gained her trust. When she was sitting on his lap and he was 'dancing,' the mom was watching and actually smiled at them, so Bella was unclear as to whether or not what Byron was doing was wrong.

"1 out of 5 children are sexually assaulted while on the Internet." - www.d2l.org

This is why it is so important for us to know what molestation entails. Parents, you are the first line of defense in preventing molestation. You have to know what it is that you are protecting your child from.

Take action now!

What will you say to start the discussion?

Chapter 3

When Should I Begin the Discussion?

"Childhood should be carefree, playing in the sun; not living a nightmare in the darkness of the soul"
- Dave Pelzer, *A Child Called "It"*

If I frightened you with the scenarios, it was not of malicious intent. Unfortunately, those scenarios are occurring in homes and in families all over the world, at this very moment! I love children so much, and I believe that they all should be protected—by any means necessary. I am allowing myself to become completely transparent with the hopes of preventing child molestation, globally. No child deserves to live with the guilt and shame of molestation.

According to the U.S. Department of Justice, most sexual abuse happens to children between the ages of 7 and 13 years old.

There is no "appropriate" age that I can recommend you to begin this conversation, but if I had to make a suggestion: I would say the earlier, the better. I have friends who had their first encounter with molestation while they were still in diapers. I was about 5 years old. My brother was 4. Part of the conversation is about empowerment, and empowerment can begin at birth.

In order for the conversation to be effective, it is going to have to be in parts, and it has to be ongoing.

You may not want to start the conversation with these scenarios if you are starting with a 4-year-old. You have to take into consideration the age and maturity of the child. It is going to take work on your part, but the positive outcomes will be well worth your efforts.

If you are having some difficulty with when to begin the discussion of molestation with your child, consider this: parents are reading to their children in the womb. The womb! It is their belief that the child hears what is being read to them and may give them a head start in learning. Parents are teaching their babies to read when they are one year old. I was one of those parents. I believed that my children would be able to read at an early age because of it. If we believe (and know) that a child can remember what he or she hears and sees, why don't we believe that a child can handle an open, honest conversation about molestation?

We teach our children to look both ways before crossing the street. We demonstrate how to safely cross the street. We ask them if they understand. We quiz them and wait for them to give us the appropriate response. We even stand back and instruct them to give us a return demonstration on how to safely cross the street. We do not stop until they get it right. Why? Because we want to prevent them from being hit by an oncoming car. Well, did you know that a child is more likely to be molested than be hit by a car?

According to the Centers for Disease Control (CDC), a child has a 1 out of 5 chance of being hit by a car by the age of 15, and 1 out of 3 girls will be molested by the age of 18. It seems that, if we want to prevent molestation, every parent will discuss molestation as vehemently and with as much effort and love as we discuss how to safely cross the street.

Take action now!

What will you say to start the discussion?

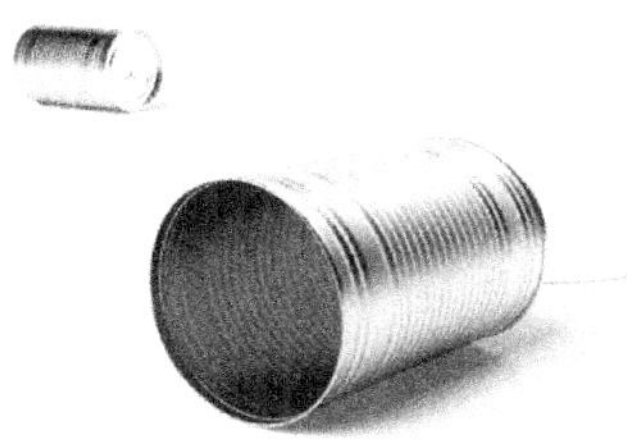

Chapter 4

What if My Child is Under 5 Years Old?

"Train up a child in the way he should go: and when he is old, he will not depart from it." - Proverbs 22:6

If you are going to have this conversation with a child who is 5 years old or younger, it is important that you do not talk overtly about sex. They may not be ready to handle the sex talk just yet. Here is where empowerment is crucial.

The reason that predators have any degree of success in molesting children without getting caught is that they prey on a child's innocence and vulnerability.

According to Family Watchdog, a child molester molests 117 times before ever being caught. They know that parents are not at home coaching their children to protect themselves. They know that the overprotective "Mama Bear" type is doing everything within her power to keep the evil of the world away from her cub. That is what they are counting on. Counter their attack and approach by giving your child the power!

Start off by telling them that their body is theirs, and they have the right to do with it what they want, as long as they do not hurt anyone. Ask them to give you examples of things that are okay to do with their body. Ask them to name the parts that are okay to touch others with. Be sure to use the anatomically correct names for body parts.

I know, you are cringing right now, but the predators are not going to be so gentle with a child. Their main goal is sexual gratification. Remember that. Get them to begin to think of their bodies as something that belongs to them so you get the wheels to begin to turn in the direction of what types of things are acceptable to do with their bodies. Enter understanding, appreciation, and power!

"Approximately 20% of the victims of sexual abuse are under the age of eight." - U.S. Department of Justice

Let me give you a scenario. This is only one approach. Feel free to add, subtract, multiply, and/or divide this scenario as you wish in order to fit your particular situation.

Your child is with you one afternoon. The day is not hurried; you do not have any practices or games of any sort to attend. It is just a relaxing afternoon, and you are just hanging out. Start out by having a casual conversation about things that you love and that make you happy: "Hey, I love my body! I am so happy to have this skin color and this eye color. Look at my hands. I love them because they are mine! What do you think about your body?" You listen as your child tries to please you, and they start to talk. As they tell you about their body, tell them, "You know that is your body, right?" Play a little game and pull their finger and say that it is their finger. You know, get them to yell, "Mine!" as they will inevitably do. Keep it light and surrender to them.

Maybe the conversation can end there, for now. If you are feeling comfortable, continue by telling them that their body is theirs and that they do not have to let anyone touch them. Remember to talk to them using verbiage that is age-appropriate. If you get too advanced, you will lose them, and they will start to talk about the next cartoon that they are hoping to watch. If that happens, approach the subject at a later time.

Maybe for the next conversation, you just walk up to them and say, "My hand!" and touch their hand. As they yell and inform you that it is not your hand, laugh and tell them that you know. Let them know that if someone touches them, and they do not like the way that it feels, that they should say, **"Don't touch me!"** Let them know that it is okay to have a conversation with someone and not touch them. Let them know that you do not have to touch someone to show them that you love them.

Give them examples of people who you love and that you do not touch: a neighbor, a cashier at a store that you frequent, a friend, or your favorite barista. Let them know that it is completely acceptable to love someone and not touch them. Give them examples of when a touch does not equal love, like in a fight. The reason for doing this is that predators are most often someone whom the child knows and is quite familiar with.

Ninety percent of child sexual abuse victims know the perpetrator in some way. The predator may try to use love to get the child to allow them to touch them (your child), so it is important that you teach them ways that love can be expressed without touch. They need to be able to say, with a strong, convincing voice, "Don't touch me! You do not have to touch me to love me! Let's go ask my mommy!"

Talk to them about secrets. Predators have been known to keep children from telling their parents or other adults about their assault because the predator told them that it was their "secret."

This is a great age to discuss what a secret is. Remind the child that if they tell you something that is supposed to be a secret, it still is. Give them examples of the type of things that are good secrets to keep. Maybe do something like this:

Ask them to define a secret to you. Once you get their definition, expound. Talk to them about good secrets, which I would call "surprises." Maybe eliminate the word secret altogether. This way, if they hear it, they know that something must be wrong. "You know how, when we shop for Christmas presents, I tell you to keep it a secret? That is because I want to see how happy the gift makes (insert a name here). If you tell them what we just bought, they will not be surprised, and we will not get a chance to see how happy they will be on Christmas Day. But even though we kept a secret, on Christmas, they found out about it. That is a good secret! It is only a secret for a little while, but then it comes out. So that is actually not a secret—it is a surprise!"

Change that scenario however you wish, but the goal is to get the child to see that a good secret (or surprise) has a positive outcome. Think of other times where secrets are fine and give them those examples in scenarios (e.g. remaining hush-hush on the sex of Mommy's unborn baby until it is born). Let the child know that it is okay to tell them any secret that someone else asked them to keep from you.

Calmly tell them that what you discuss with them is still between you and them. Let them know that they will not get into any trouble for telling you the secret. But you must stick to that! The moment they feel that telling you their secret will be punitive, they will shut down and keep it to themselves.

Let them know that it is okay to say "no" if someone tries to touch them. We should not force our children to hug or kiss anyone because we are trying to be polite or are afraid that the person will be offended. We want to teach our children about boundaries and the importance of respecting those boundaries once they have been established. There may be a reason for a child refusing to hug or kiss a certain family member.

Teach them ways to greet people, politely, which do not involve touching them. Others should not find it offensive if a child decides to use a wave and a smile as their preferred method of greeting people.

Take action now!

What will you say to start the discussion?

Chapter 5

How Do I Have "The Talk" if My Child is Between 7 to 10 Years Old?

"When to have sex, and with whom, should be the child's choice!"

If your child is in this age bracket, the conversation may shift a bit. Although the focus should still be on empowerment, the verbiage may change. It is vital that you have good communication in order to create a safe space where your child feels like he or she can come to you and talk to you about anything. When you are having this conversation with your child, work hard to keep the conversation light.

If you seem angry or upset while you are having this conversation, you run the risk of imbedding that image in their head, as it relates to molestation.

"50% of all victims of forcible sodomy, sexual assault with an object, and forcible fondling are under the age of twelve years old." - www.d2l.org

The predator may already be counting on using the manipulative tactic of guilt to keep the child quiet: "You know, this is just between us. If you tell your mommy, she is going to be very upset."

Now, the child is remembering your talk and does not want to upset you. Your goal here is to remind the child that you are their biggest advocate, and they can talk to you about anything. Again, use the anatomically correct names for body parts. "You know, you are 8 years old, and you are a big girl! You do not need anyone else to wash your vagina for you. When you wash it yourself, you do a great job!" Using the appropriate language will allow the child to understand their bodies and give them the proper terminology for use if they hear those terms or need to report suspicious behavior to a safe adult.

"14 percent of the victims of molestation reported to law enforcement agencies were under the age of six." - Bureau of Justice Statistics, 2000

To prevent molestation, there needs to be a consistent conversation. With so many cases of sexual assault in the media, there are ample opportunities to bring up the discussion. Maybe try this:

Choose a case that is, or has been, publicized where a child was molested and they reported it. It is important that you choose a case where the perpetrator received some sort of punishment, preferably imprisonment. Ask the child if they know why the perpetrator was arrested. Discuss what the person did to cause them to be arrested. Discuss how it was reported. "Wow, that person was arrested for attempting to have sex with a child. Do you believe that they should have been arrested? I wonder how the police found out about it. Do you think that the child told their parent(s) what was going on, and they called the police? That kid is really a brave little person! I am so proud of him/her! If someone touched your vagina/penis, would you tell me? If someone did something that made you feel uncomfortable, would you tell me?

Adults or big kids who touch a little kids' penis or vagina have a problem. The little kids did not do anything wrong. The adult needs some help, and when the police take them away, they will be able to get the help that they need. That kid is my hero! You know, you can tell me if someone touches you or makes you feel uncomfortable, and we will take care of it."

Once you plant the seed, listen to your child. They may be trying to analyze past acts to ascertain whether or not they have been molested. They may ask questions that do not seem to make sense to you. Listen to them. Here, you have the opportunity to establish the type of relationship that facilitates open communication. The child will sense that they can talk to you about anything, and you will take them seriously. That is vital in fostering a relationship with a child where he or she feels that they can come to you to talk to you about anything.

Listen to them and try to keep your response as positive and supportive as you possibly can. Let them know that if someone does try to touch their vagina or penis, or if they feel uncomfortable with any behavior that someone displays towards them, you want to know immediately, and they would not get into any type of trouble. This is imperative. It will not be an effective model for preventing molestation if children do not feel comfortable sharing with a safe adult—YOU!

Pay attention to their special relationships. Know who their friends are and what kind of games they play. Older kids may use game time as their opportunity to accomplish their mission. When they discuss the kinds of games that they play, inquire about the rules and participants.

Your child comes in from play. "Hey, how was playtime? What did you guys do? Wow, that sounds like fun! Who did you play with?" Use this time to give them some rules of engagement to keep them safe. Encourage them to play games in groups or around adults who will be able to supervise the children. Let them know that older children usually want to play with children their own age, and if an older child suggests playing a game alone with them, it is okay to play that game near an adult.

Be sure to ask the child questions to make sure that they comprehend what you are saying:

- What if an adult touches you, and it made you feel weird?
- What would you do?
- Would you tell anyone?
- Who?
- What if someone offered you money or a new game if you did something that Mommy said

not to do?

- What would you say to them?
- Would you do it?
- Would you tell anyone about it?

At this point, listen carefully to their responses. If they are still not sure how to handle these scenarios, be supportive. Reinforce what you have been discussing with them. "Remember, when we talked about this, we said that you can tell Mommy anything, and I will not be angry with you. It is not your fault." Always remind them that it is not their fault.

Let your child know that adults are not always right and that it is okay to say no. Give them examples of how to say no without being disrespectful. "No, I do not want to sit in your lap. Can I sit beside you?" "No, I do not need help with bathing. Thank you anyway." Hearing these examples may make them comfortable with using the word "no" appropriately and gives them power over their own body. Let them know that if they ever have any questions about how to handle any situation that they find themselves in, they can always ask you for your help with it. And be supportive.

At this age, you should probably discuss Internet safety. About 1 out of 5 children have been sexually solicited on the Internet, and 1 out of 2 children have been exposed to sexually explicit material on the Internet. Do those statistics frighten you as much as they frighten me? Because of those statistics, we have to be sure to be vigilant with monitoring our children's Internet usage.

- ✓ Have them surf the Internet or do their homework in a central location that is high-traffic and may have frequent monitoring.

- ✓ Check the sites that they surf. Place parental blocks on sites that are not age appropriate.

Because so many of our children have cell phones, we have to include cell phones in our monitoring. All kinds of things are being accessed on cell phones.

Have you noticed that Facebook is allowing soft porn to be posted onto Facebook pages?

- ✓ Check their cell phones periodically.
- ✓ Check the sites that they search.
- ✓ Check text messages that they send/receive

randomly.

If you perform random checks, it will cause them to think twice about what they view, or allow to be viewed, on their cell phones.

Take action now!

What will you do to ensure internet safety?

____

____

____

____

____

____

____

Chapter 6

How Do I Have "The Talk" if My Child is 11 Years Older or Older?

"The world is a dangerous place, not because of those who do evil, but because of those who look on and do nothing." - Albert Einstein

Talking to your children at this age can be tricky. At this age, children may not be so receptive to advice from their parents. By now, they tend to want more autonomy and just say "okay" to any conversations that we attempt to have with them in an effort to silence us so that they may go about their merry little ways.

If you are having the conversation for the first time at this stage, your approach has to be as calculated as a potential predator. Since our children have the tendency to think that they cannot trust us with their secrets at this stage, we must establish trust. Reassure your child that you can be trusted.

One way to reassure a child that you can be trusted is to inform them that they will not get in trouble if they confess something to you in order to keep them safe.

"You know, if someone touches you and it makes you feel uncomfortable, you can tell me—even if it feels good to you. It is natural for the body to respond in certain ways when it is touched, but that does not make the touch acceptable. You do not have to worry that I will become upset with you or punish you because it may have given you a little pleasure. The touch/act was wrong, and we will deal with that, together."

You may have to have several conversations with your child at this stage in order to gain their trust. Unfortunately, by the time our children reach this stage, we have been somewhat inconsistent with them and, as a result, they do not trust us. Your job is to reassure them that you can be trusted. Another way to gain their trust is to be approachable. By being open and honest with your child, you become a safe place where they feel comfortable sharing their thoughts without worrying about whether or not they will get into trouble for sharing them. When they ask you questions, give them honest, accurate, and respectful responses. But be calm. If they ask you a question and see you becoming upset, it may cause them to abruptly end the conversation. Your child does not want to be the cause of your anger or disappointment. This may cause your child to keep things to themselves. This is what you want to prevent. Be honest but calm when your child comes to you for advice and clarity.

You have to give them concrete examples. Ambiguity may be more comfortable for you when discussing molestation with your child, but it could be costly. Being clear and using correct verbiage in scenarios will help your child if, or when, they are in a situation that could lead to sexual assault or molestation. At this stage, our children's social calendar is more packed than ours! Our children are routinely being invited to sleepovers. After we have done our due diligence by ensuring that our children are going to a safe environment, we have to arm them with the tools to protect themselves. Ask them how they would handle themselves in certain situations. Here, it would be beneficial to start the conversation using the "What if?" format.

What if you saw someone stealing at Wal-Mart? What

would you do? The purpose of starting the conversation this way instead of going straight to the questions directly related to molestation is that it gives you some insight into what your child would do in unfavorable situations. Whatever their response, be mindful of not making them feel shame or guilt in their answer. If the conversation turns into a punitive or embarrassing one, your child may not want to continue answering your "What if?" questions. Make them feel that they can tell you anything without causing them to feel awful about their response.

Once you ask a few non-molestation related "What if?" questions, ask them about molestation:

- What if your best friend's 18-year-old brother asked you for a kiss? What would you do?
- What would you do if Uncle Johnny asked you to sit on his lap? What would you do?
- What would you do if you were playing and an adult asked you to kiss someone, and they watched?
- What would you do if your uncle asked you to come over to his house to babysit your little cousin, and when you walked in, he was

having sex with his door open?

- What would you do if your uncle kissed you and rubbed you on your chest but told you not to tell anyone?

Of course, you may not want to shoot the questions at them like they are in a batting cage. Those are just sample questions. Again, listen to their responses and try to remain open-minded, regardless of how they answer the question(s). Your responses are key in the empowerment of your child. I cannot reiterate that enough.

I realize at this point, some of you may be learning of your child's molestation (or attempted molestation). I cannot truly prepare you for this revelation. It is a conversation that I am sure all parents want to avoid. When my children began to discuss their molestation with me, I just listened. Because of my own experiences, my facial expressions were those of pain, sadness, and disbelief. But I listened. I believe that because I was quiet and supportive, my children continued to tell me of the times that they were molested. Sure, my heart dropped to my toenails, and I stopped breathing for a few seconds, but my reaction was a matter of life and death—my children's. I could have caused my children to shut down and suffer in silence, but instead, I created a safe zone. Remember that.

As painful as it may be to hear that your child has been molested (or approached by a predator), they need for you to be okay. Children are special that way. They try to protect us from pain and disappointment even though we are the ones who are supposed to be protecting them.

Now that we know how to talk to our children about molestation, what do we do if they confess an incident of molestation to us?

Chapter 7

How Can I Tell if a Child Has Been Molested?

"Silence is the most powerful scream." - Unknown

Unfortunately, some parents may not start the conversation about molestation until it has already occurred. If the child has not been empowered to tell a trusted adult about their encounter, they may be suffering in silence. When my children were suffering in silence, I did not know what it looked like when a child had been molested. Even though I was once that child, I could not tap into my past behaviors and identify them in either of my children. In hindsight, I had many indicators pointing to molestation in my home, but my ignorance caused me to be blind to it all.

"1 in 7 incidents of sexual assault perpetrated by juveniles occurs on school days in the after-school hours between 3 and 7pm, with a peak from 3 to 4pm." - www.d2l.org

When you read the signs of molestation, please remember that not all of these signs point to molestation, but they may point to something worth investigation—"where there's smoke, there's fire."

Just being aware of these signs may allow you to pay more attention to what is going on in your child's life and ask the questions that will help you find out what is going on.

We need to recognize the signs in order to help protect our children against molestation. The signs listed on the following pages do not necessarily point to molestation. They do, however, serve as occurrences or points worth investigating. They serve only as a guide.

1. **A child who engages in sexual conversation, activities with toys and/or people**

   You know, that child that may be a little too provocative in their manner of dress and conversation. I was raised in the South, and we called that "fast." We would say, "Look at her! She is being so fast! Get somewhere and sit your fast tail down!" That is what I heard for most of my life. It's the little girl who consistently has to be the center of attention. She is the little girl that gets told to stay out of "grown folks' business." She is the first to get up and dance in front of the crowd when a song comes on, oftentimes gyrating. She speaks of "boyfriends," regardless of her age. Always into something. I see you nodding. That's her. You know her.

Remember, she is 1 out of 3 girls, according to statistics. She is in your family, maybe in your home. You probably dismissed this behavior as nothing concerning. She is just being "fast." But think about this: little girls are not born sexy. They are "sugar and spice and everything nice." Sexy is taught and/or a learned behavior. So instead of looking at that little girl and judging her (because that is what we do), try to figure out where she got those behaviors.

Being introduced to sex by way of molestation can do some strange things to a little girl—except allow her to remain an innocent little girl.

2. A child who starts to engage in self-harming behaviors

This is the sign that went completely over my head. My son was having, what he described to me as, skateboarding accidents. He would come home from school with a bandage on his left hand. I would see it all wrapped up and believed the skateboarding accident story.

One day, the school nurse called me and said that my son comes to her office quite often to get his hand wrapped. She wanted to let me know that she did not mind wrapping his hand, but that the frequency of his visits to her office was concerning to her. I thanked her for the call and hung up the phone. Once my son came home from school, I began to accuse him of finding any reason that he could to get out of class and instructed him to never do it again (in a loud, convincing voice).

Had I been aware of the signs of molestation and what to do when I observed such signs, I would have had a conversation (or two) with my son—one where I encouraged him to share what it was that he was trying to cut out of his life through his hands.

3. **A child/teen who always has a boyfriend or girlfriend**

You notice that your daughter always has a boyfriend. A few months prior to that discovery, your daughter was focused on her schoolwork and making good grades. She played sports and was concerned and excited about her future. One day, she starts talking to you about boys. Not just one boy; now, she is interested in dating, and then you discover that she is having sex. She has multiple sex partners and is not trying to hide her sudden onset of promiscuity.

She begins to dress provocatively, and one evening, you smell alcohol on her breath. What caused the sudden change? Does she have a new teacher? Did she attend a sleepover with a friend who has an older brother or a dad who lives with them? Have the coaches of her team changed? What happened to cause this drastic change in this child?

4. **An older child who begins to act like a younger child**

You walk into your 10-year-old's room to wake him up for school, and you notice that his bed is wet. You ask him about it, and he tells you that he had a bottle of water before bed, and it was an accident. That seems like a reasonable explanation for the isolated incident of bed-wetting, so you let it go. You begin to think back and remember that you have had an increase in the number of bed sheets that you have washed. Where are all the extra sheets coming from? What is going on in that child's life that has caused them to regress?

5. **Your child refuses to be alone with someone (adult or child)**

When you have noticed this behavior, you probably thought that your child was being difficult or throwing a tantrum. For example, your child really used to enjoy going over to their Grandma's house; it seemed like every weekend, they were chomping at the bit to go see her. They started bugging you mid-week to take them to Grandma's house. Their favorite uncle is there, and he is such a big kid. But one day, your child asks if they can stay at the neighbor's house while you visit Grandma. You think nothing of it because all of the neighborhood children are outside playing and having a ball. Then, the next holiday comes around, and everyone is gathered together at Grandma's house. When Uncle Donnie comes into the room, you instruct your child to "go and give Uncle Donnie a big hug and a kiss." Your child looks at you and reluctantly does as they are instructed. Maybe there is a reason that your child is so hesitant about hugging Uncle Donnie. Why the sudden change? Maybe you should not make them hug him and ask questions to see what happened to cause the change in behavior towards their beloved Uncle Donnie.

6. Your child often complains about an illness without an obvious cause

I had to say "without an obvious cause" because, although molestation is definitely something that can make a child sick, it is not always obvious. Your child is normally a healthy child; they have only gone to the doctor in order to have their wellness checks done. If your child has a runny nose, they insist that they are okay and will not let you convince them to stay home from school. One day, the child starts to complain of a stomachache. You let them stay home from school and give them the ginger ale and Pepto combo and take care of them that day. Over the next few weeks, you start to get calls from the school nurse, and she is saying that your child has an earache one day, a headache the next week, their stomach hurts another day, and they have a sore throat a couple of weeks after that. Once you pick the child up from school, they appear to be well again. Once they are with you, they show no signs of any type of illness. Why is your child sick so often, all of a sudden? Is something happening at school that you should be aware of? Ask yourself, am I missing something?

7. A child with physical signs of abuse

Consider this scenario: One day while you are doing your family's laundry, you find a pair of your son's underwear that has streaks of blood in them. Your son is 8 years old. He has not mentioned having any type of accident/injury that would cause him to have blood in his underwear. You begin to think back, trying to figure out how he got blood in his underwear, and you remember that he had a fall last week. The next time that you do laundry, you notice another pair of blood-streaked underwear. Has he had another accident? What type of accident could your son have had that would cause him to have bloody underwear? You think back and remember that you heard him moaning when he was trying to have a bowel movement one day last week. Has someone violated this child?

8. A child with a new, older friend who gives them gifts and/or money

In this case, it could be a babysitter or an aunt or uncle who has deemed your child to be the "favorite." You notice that your child has the video game that you refused to buy or the newest pair of Jordan sneakers that you would not stand in line to buy. When you ask where he got the items, he tells you, "Tracy's dad bought them for me!" You are appreciative of the gesture and think nothing of it. After all, Tracy's dad Michael is good friends with your husband, and he coaches boys' soccer. Michael always has children—little boys—around him. "He sure does have a way with children," you think to yourself. But why is that? Why does Michael always have little boys around, whom he buys expensive gifts for? "Keep our little secret" gifts, perhaps?

Take action now!

What will you say to start the discussion?

____

____

____

____

____

____

____

____

____

____

____

Chapter 8

How Do I Respond if I Discover that My Child Has Been Molested?

"Children are a gift from the Lord: they are a reward from Him." - Psalms 127:3 KJV

As a parent of three children who were molested, this is probably where I put on a game face that you would not believe! I do not know how I did it but by the Grace of God. It is imperative to this child's well-being that you handle this appropriately. Here's the thing: I cannot give you a sure-fire way to get this right. What I can say is that **your initial reaction should be a calm one.** You absolutely must maintain your composure. You would not want the child to see you emotional or upset because they do not want to cause Mommy or Daddy any type of pain—ever! You want to give the child your undivided attention as they share their account(s).

"Child molestation is one of the most underreported crimes: only 1%-10% of molestations are ever reported." www.parentsformeganslaw.org

As they are talking, encourage them along the way: "I am so proud of you! You are such a strong little girl! You can do this!" Remind them that they have nothing to be ashamed of and that they are not the only little child who this has happened to. Assure them that the predator is the bad person and not them.

Call the local authorities. They will come out and file a report. In addition to having the report on file for future use, your child sees that you are doing something to protect them, and that may put their mind at ease about whether or not the predator will make good on their promise to kill their pet or hurt their Mommy or Daddy. Your child needs to feel protected. It is at this point that many survivors are lost. They told someone about their molestation, and no one did anything to protect them, so they grew into adults who continued to attempt to drown out the pains of their past in the most destructive of ways. Make your child feel protected and make sure they know that you are their biggest advocate!

Do not try to take matters into your own hands. Don't do it. I totally understand how hard this may be for you to do, but do not confront the predator. I know that you would be tempted to say or do something, especially if you are relatively close to the predator. But please don't do anything. You are not in a controlled environment, and things could possibly go awry, which could do you more harm than good.

You should keep the child away from the predator. They should not have to be re-victimized. That is often as painful, if not more, than the original act. Follow up on your case with the authorities in order to make sure that something is done with or to the predator. But be aware of this: it may be a slow process with an outcome that is less than desirable for you and your family. We are fighting to get tougher laws to protect our children against molestation. Do not let the low prosecution statistics keep you from reporting. Even though seeing justice being served in the molestation of your child is important, the reporting is more about letting your child know that they are safe, and that is how we can change the trajectory of our child's life after molestation!

Seek counseling for your child. Although there appears to be a stigma attached to getting professional help from a counselor to deal with issues, you have to go to counseling. It is difficult to do this without some assistance. Many of us are survivors ourselves, and it hits too close to home for us to be truly objective and effective. You did your part. It really is acceptable to allow someone who is trained in dealing with children who have been molested to assist your child on the pathway to healing. Seek a counselor with experience in the area of molestation. You may be able to contact your local Social Services or Child Protective Services to find a list of professionals who specialize in dealing with molestation. It is okay to reach out for support. Your child deserves it!

Now you have to **breath and trust the process**. This is easier said than done, but remember, I went through it. Counseling does not guarantee a quick fix. Your child is dealing with some pretty heavy stuff, even if they were not penetrated. Allow the child to go through the natural steps in the healing process. There may be some days where your child is perfectly fine and others where they may be withdrawn. That is to be expected.

Do the things that you would normally do with your child. Do not alter your routine. Your child needs to feel that things are back to normal to help them feel normal. Respect their boundaries and offer love and support as they heal. They *will* heal. With your love, support, and protection, healing will be inevitable!

Take action now!

What will you say to start the discussion?

CALL TO ACTION!

"I come as one, but I stand as 10,000!"
- Maya Angelou

Thank you for reading this book! I realize that this may not have been an easy read for some of you, but it is necessary. I believe that if parents and professionals responsible for caring for children are armed and educated about how to prevent and identify molestation, we are in a better position to prevent it!

Children cannot do this alone. Why should they have to? It is our responsibility to protect them, and we cannot do that if we do not know what we are protecting them against.

"The talk" should be the lifestyle. We cannot prevent this epidemic with one conversation over dinner. All adults that our children encounter should know what to look for and what the next steps are if they identify a child who has been molested.

It is not enough if a child hears how to protect themselves at school, but when they get home, their mom makes them hug Uncle Johnny just because she said so. We all must be on the same sheet of music in order to protect our babies!

Now that you have read the guide on how (and why) to discuss molestation with our children, **what are you waiting for?**

Let's go protect our babies! #BeatMolestation

GET HELP!

If you would like more information about how to discuss molestation with your child, visit my website: **www.DontTouchMe.org**.

If you suspect that a child may have been molested, contact your local Child Protective Services or contact Stop It Now! at 1-888-PREVENT (888-773-2362).

Other helpful resources:

The Childhelp National Child Abuse Hotline
1-800-4-A-CHILD (800-422-4453)
www.childhelp.org

Darkness to Light
1-(866) FOR-LIGHT
www.d2l.org

Rape, Abuse and Incest National Network
1-(800) 656-HOPE (4673)
www.rainn.org

Centers for Disease Control and Prevention

1-(800)-CDC-INFO (800-232-4636)

www.cdc.gov

Stop It Now

1-(888) PREVENT

www.stopitnow.org

National Suicide Prevention Lifeline

1-(800) 273-TALK

National Suicide Crisis Hotline

1-(800) SUICIDE (784-2433)

Speaking Out About Rape, Inc. (SOAR)

(321) 278-5246

www.soar99.org

ABOUT THE AUTHOR

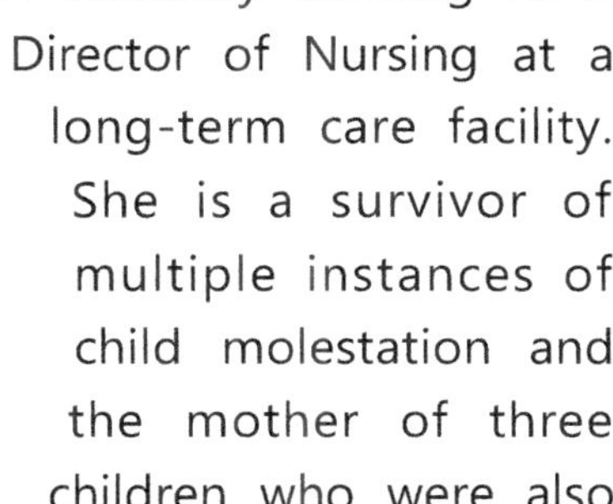

Mishondy Wright-Brown is a registered nurse who currently working as a Director of Nursing at a long-term care facility. She is a survivor of multiple instances of child molestation and the mother of three children who were also victims.

She is an author, motivational speaker, activist, and super-survivor! She believes that 95 percent of molestation is preventable and is on a mission to educate all who interact with children in any way. Her mission is to educate, inspire, and empower!

In addition, to raise awareness of molestation, Ms. Wright-Brown hosts an Annual 5k Fun Walk/Run in September at the National Harbor Mall in Washington, DC. In her spare time, she is perfecting her line of natural skin care products called Love, Me with a mission to inspire others to FLY (First.Love.Yourself)!

Visit www.DontTouchMe.org to learn more

We use the following hashtags on social media:

#MyBodyMyChoice

#BeatMolestation

#DontTouchMe

#DontTouchMe5k

#NoMoreSecretsBook

WE WANT TO HEAR FROM YOU!!!

If this book has made a difference in your life Mishondy would be delighted to hear about it.

Leave a review on Amazon.com!

BOOK MISHONDY TO SPEAK AT YOUR NEXT EVENT!

Send an email to: booking@publishyourgift.com

LEARN MORE AT:

www.DontTouchMe.org

FOLLOW MISHONDY ON SOCIAL MEDIA

 DontTouchMe2013  iamDontTouchMe

"EMPOWERING YOU TO IMPACT GENERATIONS"

WWW.PUBLISHYOURGIFT.COM

CPSIA information can be obtained at www.ICGtesting.com
Printed in the USA
BVOW06s1100070316

439296BV00006B/2/P